SIMON HILTON

The Product Culture Pyramid

Building a Principles-Driven Product Culture

Copyright © 2023 by Simon Hilton

All rights reserved. No part of this publication may be reproduced, stored or transmitted in any form or by any means, electronic, mechanical, photocopying, recording, scanning, or otherwise without written permission from the publisher. It is illegal to copy this book, post it to a website, or distribute it by any other means without permission.

First edition

*This book was professionally typeset on Reedsy.
Find out more at reedsy.com*

Contents

I Introduction

1 Cultural Foundations   3
2 Who Is This For?   6

II The Role of Culture

3 What Is Culture?   11
4 What About Product Culture?   14
5 Context and Collaboration   17
6 The Effects of Bad Product Cultures   20

III Good Culture Outcomes

7 Building a Good Culture   25
8 Guidance   28
9 Trust Is Earned, Not Given   31
10 Coaching   34
11 Principles   37
12 Assessing Your Product Culture   40

IV The Framework

13	It Starts With a Strong Operating Model	47
14	Quality	51
15	Urgency	55
16	Impact	58
17	Crafting Your Principles	61
18	Steal Like an Artist	64
19	Write It Down and Share It.	67

V Conclusion

20	Maintaining a Product Culture	73
21	Appendix - Principles Example	76

About the Author	79
Also by Simon Hilton	80

I

Introduction

1

Cultural Foundations

Many years ago, I found myself in the role of Head of Product at a thriving SaaS company. It was an exhilarating position filled with challenges and opportunities. However, as the company continued to grow, a peculiar challenge emerged - product operations. The inefficiencies and struggles within this critical function were becoming increasingly apparent. It was clear that we needed a more systematic approach to tackle these issues.

There was a lot of confusion due to different sources of information. This led to teams, including the product team, spending more time trying to understand what was being built and why, instead of focusing on how they could work together to make it happen. There was also a sense of uncertainty about the process and the decisions being made. We found ourselves dealing with an abundance of opinions, but we lacked methods that were based on solid evidence.

In my quest to enhance our product operations, I embarked on a journey to find valuable resources and insights. Much to my surprise, there was a noticeable scarcity of high-quality materials on this subject. Determined to make a difference and contribute to the product management community, I decided to create content that could shed light on the intricacies of product operations. This decision marked the beginning of my work to craft what I would later call the "Product Ops Pillars."

However, as I delved deeper into the realm of product operations, a crucial realisation emerged: no matter how flawlessly you execute your operations, success is ultimately determined by your strategic direction. It's like rowing a boat with all your might, but if you're heading in the wrong direction, it doesn't matter how hard you work. This revelation led me to co-author "Product Strategy Bridge" with my partner in this journey, Alejandro Patterson. Together, we demystified the complex world of product strategy, offering clarity and actionable insights to fellow product managers.

Yet, as I continued to explore the fascinating landscape of product management, a persistent question gnawed at me: Why aren't more product managers embracing these strategic behaviours? What is holding them back from unlocking their full potential?

Could Product Culture be the key that unlocks the door to excellence in product operations and strategy? Can it serve as the driving force behind a thriving and innovative product team? Questions like these ignited my curiosity that set me on a path of discovery.

In the following chapters, we'll discuss the importance of

Product Culture in product management. We'll examine its effects and how it contributes to superior product operations and strategies.

2

Who Is This For?

Let's start by identifying who this book is made for. If you find yourself in the exciting and dynamic role of a product leader within a SaaS company that has already achieved the elusive state of product-market fit, then you're in the right place. This book is designed with you in mind.

As a product leader in such a company, you bear the weighty responsibility of steering the ship toward success. You oversee multiple teams, each contributing to the overall outcome, and you understand how these outcomes directly impact your target customers. It's a thrilling, yet challenging, role—one that demands a unique set of skills and knowledge.

Unlike other lengthy and theoretical books on product management, this one stands out by being practical, concise, and actionable. It aims to provide a clear direction for implementing Product Culture principles in your organisation.

Appreciating the value of your time and the multitude of tasks you juggle, this book is designed to be straightforward and efficient. It avoids unnecessary digressions and focuses on clear, actionable steps that you can start applying right away.

However, if you happen to be part of a company that has not yet achieved product-market fit, I recommend exploring lean methodology books that cater to a more scrappy and experimental approach. Building a solid Product Culture is a worthy pursuit, but it's most effective when you have a proven product-market fit to build upon.

So, if you're a product leader in a SaaS company that's achieved product-market fit and you're eager to enhance your organisation's performance, you're in the right place. This book is your roadmap to unlocking the potential of Product Culture and driving your teams towards even greater success. Let's dive in and make it happen!

II

The Role of Culture

3

What Is Culture?

In the world of business, the term "culture" often gets thrown around, but what exactly does it mean, and why is it so crucial to the success of your organisation?

Culture, in its essence, is the invisible yet omnipresent force that shapes the way people work together within an organisation. It's a blend of collective values, beliefs, behaviours, and norms that define the environment in which your teams operate. Think of it as the unwritten rules that guide everything from decision-making to collaboration. They are the behaviours that you allow or endorse and the ones you don't through your everyday actions and expectations.

One of the first steps in your journey to understanding and embracing Product Culture is recognizing that your business already has a culture of its own. It's like the DNA of your organisation, influencing how work gets done, how people interact, and what your company aspires to achieve.

To truly thrive in this culture-driven landscape, it's essential to immerse yourself in your organisation's existing culture. Understand who plays a role in shaping it and what its overarching goals and aspirations are. This knowledge will serve as a foundation as you embark on your journey to foster a Product Culture within your team and organisation.

One key context to consider within the realm of culture is whether your organisation leans towards being sales-driven or product-driven. This distinction is crucial because blindly applying product theory without recognising this can quickly strain relationships with your peers.

While your role as a product leader may entail advocating for the product, it's paramount to remember that the ultimate goal is fostering a collaborative environment across the entire organisation. The synergy between sales and product teams, among others, is what fuels growth and innovation. A harmonious balance between these two aspects of culture is essential for success.

It's worth noting that culture is not static; it's a living entity that evolves as your organisation grows and changes. When new people join, when others depart, when the size of your business shifts, or when you acquire new entities, each of these factors can have a profound impact on your organisational culture. Therefore, it's vital to constantly reassess and adapt to ensure that your culture remains aligned with your objectives and values.

As we journey deeper into the world of Product Culture, keep in mind that understanding your organisation's culture is the first step toward transforming it. With this knowledge in hand, you'll be better equipped to navigate the intricate nuances of culture and harness its power to drive positive change within your company.

4

What About Product Culture?

In the world of product development, an often underestimated but incredibly powerful force is at play – Product Culture. It's the essence of what drives successful product teams and their ability to deliver exceptional outcomes. In this chapter, we'll delve deeper into the critical role that Product Culture plays in operationalising your company culture to consistently deliver valuable outcomes to your customers through your products. We'll also explore the pivotal role of leadership in nurturing and growing a thriving Product Culture.

To grasp the concept fully, let's start with a fundamental question: What is Product Culture?

At its core, culture represents the collective values, beliefs, behaviours, and norms that shape how a group of individuals work together. Product, in the context of a product team, is the craft of shipping valuable outcomes to customers that impact their lives. When we combine these two concepts together, we get Product Culture – a unique blend of values, beliefs, behaviours, and norms that are indispensable for delivering valuable outcomes to customers.

It's worth noting that Product cultures can differ significantly on many factors including size, industry or even personal style of the leaders involved. For example a small startup could have a culture of shipping fast and in small tight knit teams whereas a large bank could require a culture of smooth and steady progress with a focus on quality. All of these have their place but all must share some essential ingredients which we will go into later in this book.

Think of it as the golden thread that guides your team through the maze of challenges, decisions, and uncertainties that come with product development. It's the compass that keeps you on course, especially when the path ahead is unclear.

But here's what makes Product Culture truly fascinating: it's not a one-size-fits-all model. It's as distinct as your organisation itself, intricately woven into how you bring those valuable outcomes to life. It's a fusion of what inherently makes your organisation special and what you uniquely contribute as a product leader.

However, the real power of Product Culture lies in its ability to drive growth and operationalize your company culture. It's not just about celebrating your strengths; it's also about recognizing where you can improve and taking your organisation from good to great. It thrives on innovation, encourages calculated risks, and treats failure as a stepping stone to success.

In essence, Product Culture is the lifeblood of your product team. It's the shared understanding of why you do what you do, the guiding principles that shape how you do it, and the core values that influence your decisions. It's the cohesive force that binds your team together, even when facing tough choices and navigating uncharted waters.

For Product Culture to flourish, it requires a leader who can advocate and guide it. A product leader plays a pivotal role in defining and reinforcing the culture within the team. They must be the torchbearer of the values, the embodiment of the beliefs, and the living example of the behaviours that deliver valuable outcomes. Without a leader who champions and nurtures Product Culture, it may remain an abstract concept rather than a tangible force that drives your team towards success.

5

Context and Collaboration

"Why aren't good product cultures easy to find?" It's a question that echoes through the minds of many product managers, and if you've been in the industry long enough, you've likely heard the stories. Tales of feeling relegated to mere feature factories or order takers, where the direction for the product is dictated rather than determined by the very people responsible for its success.

So, why does this happen, and why are product cultures that truly empower their teams so elusive?

The truth is, it all comes down to trust. Trust is the cornerstone of a robust Product Culture, and building it isn't always a straightforward path. Let's explore why.

Imagine a scenario where a product manager is handed the reins of a product, with the freedom to shape its direction. Sounds ideal, right? But here's the catch – trust must be earned, not given. Many product managers find themselves in roles where they're not entrusted with this level of responsibility because they haven't yet built up enough context and credibility.

Especially in early-stage companies, there's a wealth of context about the customer, the market, and the founder's vision that has been carefully cultivated over time. This context is invaluable when making critical product decisions. It's the foundation upon which a strong Product Culture is built.

To be entrusted with the power to shape a product's destiny, a product manager must first become a trusted collaborator. They need to accumulate the knowledge, experience, and understanding necessary to make informed decisions. This often involves a journey of learning, contributing, and demonstrating their ability to align with the broader goals of the organisation.

In essence, it's about earning a seat at the decision-making table. A product manager must showcase their value, not just as executors of tasks but as strategic thinkers who can drive the product forward. It's about proving that they can carry the weight of these decisions, understanding the implications they may have on the product, the team, and the company as a whole.

Now, here's the good news. While it may not be easy, building trust and earning the right to shape a product's destiny is entirely achievable. It's about actively seeking opportunities to contribute beyond your role, demonstrating your dedication to the product's success, and consistently delivering results.

So, don't be disheartened if you've felt like a cog in the machine. In the world of product culture, trust is the currency that opens doors, and with the right mindset and actions, you can unlock the full potential of your team and your product.

6

The Effects of Bad Product Cultures

In the world of product development, culture matters. As we've explored in previous chapters, a strong product culture can be a game-changer for your team, your product, and your customers. But what happens when your product culture takes a wrong turn or, even worse, is non-existent? In this chapter, we'll delve into the repercussions of a bad product culture, drawing from insights gathered through interviews with seasoned product leaders.

Misalignment Woes

A strong product culture begins with a distinct vision and strategy. When your team understands what they're building but lacks the critical context of its purpose and the audience it serves, a gap begins to form. This gap is like an orchestra out of sync, with the product team, leaders, and the rest of the business each playing to a different rhythm.

Consider a ship without a map or compass—it's destined to meander aimlessly. In the same vein, without a clear vision and strategic direction, your product efforts can drift into a sea of uncertainty, leaving both your team and your customers directionless. Crafting a clear vision and strategy is the first step towards building a culture that breathes this vision and is empowered to innovate within this strategic framework.

Sluggish Time to Value

Another alarming consequence of a deficient product culture is a noticeable slowdown in the Time to Value (TTV). The process becomes bogged down by layers of oversight and bureaucracy. Instead of being empowered to make swift, well-informed decisions, the team is forced to seek permission at every turn.

Picture a race car stuck in a traffic jam—it might have the potential for speed, but it's going nowhere fast. When a team is hindered by the need for constant approvals and microman-agement, the very essence of agility is compromised. Your competitors, operating with a robust product culture, will leave you in the dust, reaching the finish line long before you even get close.

Motivation Matters

Lastly, let's talk about the heart and soul of your product development team—motivation. A good product culture nurtures intrinsic motivation, that burning desire to make your customers' lives better. But when that culture is lacking, motivation becomes an elusive beast that requires constant external prodding.

Think of it as trying to light a damp campfire—it's a lot of effort for little warmth. Teams without a healthy product culture become harder to motivate. They become reliant on external stimuli, like the relentless cheerleading of leaders, rather than finding fulfilment in the meaningful impact they can have on the lives of their users.

In stark contrast, a healthy product culture can be a game-changer of its own. It thrives on alignment, where every member of the team understands not just what they're building but also who it's for and why it matters. This culture fuels speed to value, empowering teams to make decisions swiftly, ensuring that the journey to delivering customer value is as efficient as possible. And, most importantly, it cultivates intrinsic motivation, lighting a fire within each team member to tirelessly pursue the goal of making their customers' lives better. So, as we explore the path to building a robust product culture in the following chapters, remember that the rewards are profound—a team firing on all cylinders, a product that resonates with users, and customers who are delighted by the value you provide.

III

Good Culture Outcomes

7

Building a Good Culture

In the exciting world of product development, there's a secret sauce that can transform your team and organisation.

The Sweet Spot: Less Control, More Empathy

Imagine a work environment where you don't have to constantly crack the whip or keep an eagle eye on your team to ensure they're on the right track. Picture a scenario where your team members are not just meeting your expectations but surpassing them, all while taking ownership of their work. Sounds like a dream, right?

This dream becomes a reality when you nurture a good product culture. In this culture, you'll find that less direct control and motivation are needed because your team members are motivated from within. They're not just following orders; they're driven by a deep sense of purpose and a genuine desire to make a difference.

Unlocking the Power of Empathy

One of the most remarkable benefits of a good product culture is that it frees up your team's mental space and energy. When they're not bogged down by constant oversight and micromanagement, they can redirect their focus to something truly transformative: empathy.

Empathy is the secret ingredient that sets exceptional product teams apart. It's about understanding your customers on a profound level, not just what they say they want, but what they truly need. A strong product culture gives your team the breathing room to connect with your customers emotionally, to walk in their shoes, and to see the world from their perspective.

Innovation Thrives in Freedom

In a culture where your team feels empowered and motivated, innovation becomes second nature. They're not constrained by rigid processes or stifling rules. Instead, they're encouraged to think outside the box, experiment with bold ideas, and push the boundaries of what's possible.

When your team doesn't need constant prodding, they're free to focus on what really matters: creating innovative solutions that resonate with your customers. They'll be more likely to take calculated risks, embrace change, and adapt quickly to evolving market dynamics.

Cultivate a Culture That Sets You Free

In the quest to build a good product culture, remember that it's not about exerting more control; it's about progressively building the strength of your team with the goal of letting them take on more of the decision making process.

Therefore, cultivating a culture that sets the team free isn't just about a hands-off approach. It's about setting clear expectations, providing the right tools, and then stepping aside to let your team do what they do best. It's about demonstrating faith in their abilities, trust in their decisions and creating a safe space for failure, learning, and growth.

8

Guidance

In the world of product development, one of the most remarkable benefits of fostering a strong product culture is that your team becomes empowered to make decisions even when you're not in the room. It's like planting seeds of motivation and trust that grow into a thriving garden of innovation and initiative. In this chapter, we'll explore why this aspect of a good product culture is so essential and how you can nurture it within your team.

The Power of Autonomous Decision-Making

Imagine a scenario where your team not only understands your vision but also possesses the confidence and know-how to make decisions aligned with that vision. This is the magic that a good product culture can bring to your organisation. When your team members have a clear understanding of the principles and values that guide your product development, they become more than just workers; they become active contributors to the bigger picture.

In a strong product culture, you won't have to micromanage every detail or provide step-by-step instructions. Instead, your team will take the initiative, make informed choices, and solve problems creatively. They'll feel a sense of ownership over their work, which is a powerful motivator. This newfound autonomy not only boosts productivity but also fosters a more vibrant and innovative work environment.

Motivation from Within

One of the most significant advantages of a team that can make decisions independently is the intrinsic motivation it generates. When team members are empowered to find their way, they no longer rely solely on external motivation. They're driven by a sense of purpose and ownership, a desire to contribute to a greater mission. This internal motivation is a sustainable force that keeps your team engaged, even in challenging times.

Think about it: instead of constantly pointing your team in the right direction and motivating them to reach their goals, you'll find them eager to chart their own course. They'll tackle problems head-on, experiment with new ideas, and seek continuous improvement, all because they're genuinely invested in the success of the product and the company.

Even with this kind of direction and energy though, teams still require course correction. We will cover this with coaching later in the book.

Building a Culture of Trust

A thriving product culture begins with sowing the seeds of trust within your team. Creating an environment that fosters trust is fundamental to empowering team members to take initiative, voice their ideas, and shoulder the responsibility of decision-making. This trust is not exclusive to the team members alone but extends to the organisation as a whole. As a product leader, you must facilitate open communication, attentively heed your team's perspectives, and offer constructive feedback.

However, trust goes hand in hand with accountability. Greater trust awarded to individuals warrants corresponding levels of accountability. These aren't antagonistic concepts; rather, they exist in a delicate balance. As team members are entrusted with more responsibility, they must understand the expectations tied to their roles and the outcomes they deliver. Ensuring these outcomes align with your business goals is crucial. Building a culture of trust and accountability doesn't just enhance team dynamics—it sets a solid foundation for an effective product culture.

9

Trust Is Earned, Not Given

In the ever-evolving world of product culture, one of the most valuable lessons you can learn is that trust is a currency earned, not given. We live in a world where everyone wants to be a decision-maker, but not everyone is willing to put in the work to earn that privilege.

The Hard Truth: Trust Must Be Earned

It's an all-too-common scenario: a new product manager enters the scene with grand visions and high expectations. They want to wield influence, make critical decisions, and guide the product's direction. But here's the reality check: trust isn't something you automatically inherit with your title or position. It's a precious commodity that must be earned through time, effort, and actions.

Building trust in the world of product management isn't just about having good ideas; it's about demonstrating a deep understanding of your domain. It's about showing that you're not just another voice in the room but a valuable team member who brings a unique perspective based on a wealth of knowledge and experience.

The Foundation of Trust: Context and Expertise

To earn trust, you must first build a solid foundation of context and expertise. This means diving headfirst into understanding your customers, the market landscape, your competitors, your business objectives, and your team's capabilities. Without this knowledge, you're simply navigating in the dark.

Take the time to immerse yourself in your product's ecosystem. Talk to customers, analyse data, study the competition, and collaborate with your colleagues. The deeper your understanding, the more credibility you'll gain. When you speak, people will know that your insights are grounded in reality, not just wishful thinking.

Show, Don't Tell: Building a Reputation

Trust isn't just about what you say; it's about what you do. To establish trust, you need to show, not tell. This means crafting a track record of delivering results and making meaningful contributions to your product and organisation's success.

Consistently develop and execute valuable plans that yield tangible outcomes. Demonstrate your ability to take an idea from concept to reality, and showcase how your decisions positively impact the product and the organisation as a whole. Your actions will speak volumes, and others will begin to look to you as a trusted guide.

The Journey to Influence

Earning trust is not a one-time event; it's an ongoing journey. As you accumulate trust through your expertise and actions, you'll find that doors to greater influence start to open. Your voice will carry more weight, your decisions will be respected, and your ability to guide your team and organisation will be acknowledged.

Remember, influence and trust are not entitlements; they are privileges earned through dedication and a commitment to excellence. Embrace this journey, and you'll discover that the more you give to your role, the more it will give back to you.

10

Coaching

In the world of product management, coaching is an essential skill, especially when you're striving to build a robust product culture within your organisation. A strong product culture not only guides your team's actions but also simplifies the coaching process for you and other leaders.

Defining Your Values

At the heart of a thriving product culture lies a set of shared values. These values serve as the compass that directs your team's decisions and actions. When you establish a clear set of values, you're essentially answering the question, "What do we value most in our product development process?" This, in turn, creates a blueprint for decision-making.

Imagine your product culture values speed and innovation above all else. When your team faces a decision that could potentially slow down the development process but increase quality, your established culture can guide them. They'll be equipped with a framework that helps them evaluate the decision in light of your core values.

A Constructive Lens for Decisions

Inevitably, there will be instances where decisions are made that seem to contradict your established product culture. This is a natural part of the process, and it's where your role as a coach becomes pivotal. Instead of viewing these deviations as roadblocks, see them as opportunities for growth and learning.

When a decision doesn't align with your product culture, approach it constructively. Engage in open conversations with your team members to understand their thought process. Why did they make that choice? What factors influenced them? This dialogue not only encourages transparency but also fosters a culture of continuous improvement.

Adapting and Updating

There will be moments when a decision falls outside your current culture because it's a novel situation. In such cases, use it as a chance to evolve and refine your product culture. Reflect on whether the existing values still hold or if they need modification.

Additionally, consider individual circumstances. Sometimes, team members may have valid reasons for their choices that you hadn't initially accounted for. Recognise and appreciate these unique situations while still upholding your core values. It's about striking a balance between maintaining cultural consistency and allowing flexibility when warranted.

Creating Shared Understanding

One of the greatest benefits of a well-defined product culture is that it fosters a shared understanding among your team members. When everyone knows what the culture stands for and how it guides decision-making, it becomes easier to navigate challenging conversations.

11

Principles

Principles, as simple as they may sound, are a powerful force in shaping behaviour and aligning decision-making. Think of them as the North Star that helps your team navigate the vast sea of choices and actions they encounter daily. You understand that a well-defined culture can set expectations and guide your team toward success. Now, let's dive into the essential step of bringing your product culture to life by crafting a set of principles.

Crafting Your Principles

Creating a set of guiding principles for your product culture is both an art and a science. It requires thoughtful consideration of what you want your team to value and when those values should be applied. These principles should reflect the essence of your product culture and capture the key tenets that drive your decision-making process.

When crafting your principles, involve your team in the process. Seek their input and feedback to ensure that these values resonate with everyone. Remember, these principles aren't just for display; they should genuinely reflect the shared beliefs and aspirations of your team.

Problem Patterns

In the realm of product development, we often face recurring challenges. We must learn to recognise these patterns, develop systematic approaches to tackle them, and, most importantly, use these challenges as opportunities for learning and improvement. Your product culture should foster a mindset that turns each decision into a pathway to continuous growth and resilience, where familiar hurdles are transformed into stepping stones for greater success

These principles serve as a mental framework that helps your team quickly identify how to approach a problem or decision. They become a shared language, a common ground that unites your team, regardless of individual differences or backgrounds. This shared understanding simplifies complex scenarios and empowers your team to act in alignment with your culture.

Guidance, Not Rules

It's important to emphasise that principles are not rigid rules meant to stifle creativity or innovation. Instead, they act as gentle guidance, providing a direction while allowing room for individual judgement. They are there to facilitate decision-making based on shared values, not to make the decision for you.

As a product leader, you should encourage your team to embrace these principles as tools for empowerment, not constraints. They should feel free to adapt and apply them in ways that best suit the specific context of a given situation. This flexibility is key to fostering a culture that values both alignment and adaptability.

In the next section, we'll explore how to start building this culture and writing your own principles, ensuring that your team thrives in an environment where values are not just words on paper, but a living, breathing part of your everyday work life.

12

Assessing Your Product Culture

As an aspiring product manager or leader, the decision to join any organisation should be underpinned by an understanding of their product culture. This understanding can be extracted by dissecting the business into our three foundational layers: Quality, Urgency, and Impact. They each require ongoing attention and reinvestment to maintain a thriving product environment.

Quality

Quality in this context addresses the company's ability to deliver high-standard and consistent product offerings to its stakeholder base.

Ask pointed questions like:

- On average, how often is your product or software deployed to production?

- In real-time, how long is the interval between code submission and its production?
- Is there a firm structure of automated tests within your CI/CD pipeline, and how reliable is this system overall?
- In a situation where post-development issues or bugs are reported by users, what measures are put in place by your team to rectify these?

These queries will provide insights into the company's approach to managing product quality as well as their commitment to upholding a high delivery standard. Inadequate answers in this space can hint that it will be hard for you to reach any sort of high velocity with your speed to market.

Urgency

Urgency reflects the team's agility and accountability in deciding what to work on and how to align other teams towards these decisions. Ask the following to assess this layer of the pyramid:

Ask questions such as:

- How does your team go about prioritising the product backlog?
- Can you walk me through the process product managers deploy in crafting their strategy for the upcoming quarter?
- Is it possible to recall an instance where a quick decision had to be made to meet a tight release deadline, and what was the outcome of the situation?

- Are there any specific methods or tools at your team's disposal to sustain alignment and adherence to roadmaps and organisational expectations?

These questions can throw light on the decision-making dynamics of the company and how agile they are in handling changing priorities.

Impact

The final layer, impact, measures the organisation's ability to select and evaluate initiatives that significantly influence strategic goals. Enquire about these aspects:

To gauge the company's impact strategies, ask:

- How does your organisation measure the return on investment (ROI) for each launched product or feature?
- Can you illustrate how the strategic vision of your product dovetails into the overall business goal?
- What level of access do your Product Managers have to essential company data like revenue, customer and product metrics for intuitive decision making?
- How are poorly performing features or products handled in terms of business impact or ROI?

These queries can give you a vivid outline of the organisation's strategic objectives and their dedication to continuous improvement, thereby giving you a clearer perspective on whether your role in the organisation can make a meaningful difference.

Remember, product culture is not a one-size-fits-all concept. Therefore, these questions are guides, and you should adapt them based on the specific company or role under consideration. Cultivating a keen understanding of the organisational culture and aligning it with your aspirations can significantly influence your contribution and satisfaction in a new role.

IV

The Framework

13

It Starts With a Strong Operating Model

Creating a robust product culture isn't solely a top-down endeavour; it's equally about empowering your team from the ground up. A crucial element in this journey is developing an effective operating model. This chapter delves into why a solid operating model is the cornerstone of momentum, enabling your team to make informed decisions and deliver exceptional outcomes for both your customers and your business.

The Power of a Good Operating Model

Imagine your product culture as a well-tuned engine. While culture provides the vision and values, the operating model is what propels it forward. It's the practical framework that translates these ideals into actionable steps. Having a well-defined operating model is like having a roadmap that guides your team to success.

Before you can excel in delivering many things, you must first master the art of shipping one thing exceptionally well. Your operating model is the tool that allows you to streamline processes, optimise workflows, and achieve this level of precision.

Earning Trust and Focus

One of the most significant advantages of a good operating model is the trust it engenders among executives and other leaders within your organisation. When your product team operates efficiently and consistently delivers value, it allows executives to step away from day-to-day management and focus on higher-leverage activities such as securing funding, forming partnerships, or exploring potential acquisitions.

By demonstrating your team's ability to execute based on a

strong operating model, you not only earn the trust of your superiors but also gain the credibility needed to tackle more significant and valuable challenges. It's a pathway to becoming a trusted advisor and strategic partner within your organisation.

As you progress through this book and begin to implement the principles of a strong product culture, remember the mantra: "Progress over perfection." Building and fine-tuning your operating model is an iterative process, and with each step forward, you bring your team closer to achieving exceptional outcomes for your customers and your business. So, embrace the journey, and let's continue to explore the building blocks of a thriving product
 culture.

The Components of a Strong Product Culture

At the core of a good product culture lie three key elements: Quality, Urgency, and Impact. These layers serve as the foundation upon which your culture is built, guiding your team's actions and decisions. In the following chapters, we'll explore each of these layers in depth and understand how they shape your culture from the ground up.

- **Quality**: Quality is not just about creating a polished product; it's about maintaining a commitment to excellence in everything you do. We'll delve into how a focus on quality can set the standard for your team's work and build trust with your customers.

- **Urgency**: Urgency is the driving force that propels your team forward. It's about recognizing the importance of time and the need to act swiftly and decisively. We'll explore how a sense of urgency can infuse your team with energy and purpose.
- **Impact**: Impact is the ultimate measure of success. It's about ensuring that your efforts result in tangible, meaningful outcomes for your customers and your business. We'll discuss how a relentless pursuit of impact can define your team's purpose and drive.

As we journey through these key layers, we'll uncover the nuances of each element and how they interact to create a thriving product culture. Remember, building a strong culture is not a destination; it's a continuous process of growth and refinement.

14

Quality

In the realm of product culture, the first layer you must solidify revolves around your delivery practices. Simply put, if you can't consistently deliver one thing with quality, your ability to handle multiple tasks and strategies will be compromised. This chapter explores the importance of a quality culture as the cornerstone of your product culture.

Quality Culture: The Foundation to Success

Quality isn't just a checkbox; it's the heartbeat of your product culture. It's the bar you set for every task and project. A quality culture means consistently meeting and exceeding customer expectations, building trust, and demonstrating your commitment to excellence.

When quality becomes an integral part of your culture, it ensures that every product, feature, or service you offer is a testament to your dedication to delivering the best possible experience to your customers.

Developer Velocity: A Crucial Predictor for Success

In the ever-evolving landscape of product development, developer velocity emerges as a powerful predictor of success. How quickly your team can conceive, build, and deliver valuable features can determine your competitive edge. It's not just about speed; it's about being responsive and adaptive in a fast-paced market.

Maintaining developer velocity should be a top priority. It's not just about the quantity of output but also the quality. A culture that values both speed and precision can enable your team to innovate rapidly without compromising on the excellence your customers expect.

The Starting Line for Your Journey

Begin by closely examining your delivery practices. Are you consistently meeting your release targets? Is the quality of your output consistently high? Are you learning and improving with each release?

Identify areas for improvement and engage your engineering teams in the process. Encourage a culture of continuous improvement, where every release is seen as an opportunity to enhance your practices.

As you refine your quality culture, you'll notice a transformation within your team. They'll become more reliable, efficient, and effective. This newfound trust in your delivery capability sets the stage for the next phase – product management, where you'll confidently shape the future of your product.

Defining Quality on Your Terms

Quality isn't one-size-fits-all; it's a concept that needs to be defined individually within your company. What constitutes quality in your context may differ from industry standards, and that's perfectly fine. The key is to strike the right balance between moving swiftly and ensuring that your product doesn't break every time a change is made.

Your quality standards should align with your unique goals, customer expectations, and the nature of your product. This approach allows you to move at the desired speed while maintaining a stable and reliable product. It's a delicate dance that requires continuous assessment and fine-tuning.

Building a good quality culture also means that you need to have strong partnerships with your engineering and design peers. Approach any improvements in a collaborative manner as a shared initiative across product, engineering and design teams as it is a cross functional responsibility where everyone needs to contribute to the outcome.

Earning the Right to Look Ahead

While the technical aspects of maintaining a quality culture often fall within the realm of your engineering teams, product leaders have a crucial role to play. Your ability to shape the future of your product relies on a strong foundation of quality delivery.

Consistency in execution is the currency of trust and credibility within your organisation. By demonstrating your team's commitment to quality and excellence, sprint after sprint, you earn the credibility and influence to explore longer-term product management strategies as you are showing the product experience matters and is in good hands.

15

Urgency

With your delivery practices operating smoothly under the watchful eye of your engineering teams and leaders, it's time to shift your focus to the realm of product management. This chapter explores the vital role of urgency in your product culture and why it's one of the most crucial qualities for a successful product team and product managers.

Urgency: The Driving Force

Throughout my career, I've learned that urgency is one of the most potent driving forces for a product team. While there are countless ways to progress your product in the market, it's your responsibility, as a product manager, to identify the most valuable and urgent opportunities and instil that sense of urgency across your organisation.

Why is urgency so important? It's because urgency fuels action. It's the force that propels your team forward, ensuring that the most critical tasks are addressed promptly and effectively. Without a sense of urgency, complacency can set in, and important opportunities may slip through the cracks.

The Key Role of Product Managers

As a product manager, you are not just a passenger on this journey; you are the driver. Your role is to identify the most pressing needs, the opportunities that can make a significant impact, and then guide your team in tackling them with urgency.

It's true that some product teams may feel they lack the authority needed to make impactful decisions. They may find themselves trapped in the "feature factory," where they simply react to requests without a clear sense of direction. However, you can break free from this cycle by consistently making good decisions about the product's direction and aligning them with the organisation's strategic goals.

Time-to-Market: The Competitive Edge

Speed to market is a critical factor in gaining a competitive edge and capitalising on opportunities. Being the first to deliver a valuable solution or feature to your target audience can set you apart from competitors and establish your product as an industry leader. It allows you to capture market share, generate revenue, and demonstrate your commitment to meeting customer needs promptly.

Time-to-market also affects revenue generation, return on investment, and overall business growth. The faster you can bring a product or feature to market, the sooner you can start generating revenue from it, and the quicker you can recover development costs.

Moreover, time-to-market aligns with customer expectations. In today's fast-paced digital landscape, customers often expect rapid updates, improvements, and new features. Failing to deliver promptly can lead to user dissatisfaction and attrition.

Earning the Right to Lead with Urgency

To instil a culture of urgency, you must lead by example. If your product team doesn't display a sense of urgency in their work, why should anyone else in your organisation? Your dedication to identifying and pursuing the most critical opportunities sets the tone for your team and inspires action at every level.

You earn the right to lead with urgency by consistently making decisions that drive the product forward, by aligning your product strategy with the company's goals, and by relentlessly pursuing valuable opportunities.

For a deeper dive into mastering the art of product strategy and building a culture of urgency, I've created a comprehensive playbook called "The Product Strategy Bridge." It provides actionable insights and practical guidance to help you become a strategic leader in your organisation.

16

Impact

As you've embraced urgency and nurtured a culture of quality, the next vital step is to translate these efforts into meaningful impact for your customers and your business. This chapter explores the essential role of impact in your product culture and why it's crucial to bridge the gap between customer focus and business mission.

Impact: The Ultimate Measure

While urgency and quality are foundational pillars of a thriving product culture, their true significance shines through when they culminate in impact. After all, the ultimate measure of success is the positive change you bring to your customers and your business. Urgency propels your team to act swiftly, ensuring that what you deliver is not just timely but also aligned with customer needs. Quality, on the other hand, guarantees that what you deliver meets the highest standards of excellence, reinforcing your customers' trust and loyalty.

The Customer Focus Trap

It's common for product teams to become so customer-centric that they lose sight of the bigger picture. While catering to customer needs is essential, it's equally crucial to ensure that your efforts align with the mission of the business and generate a return on investment for your board and investors. Impact requires a holistic perspective that encompasses both customer satisfaction and business success. Striking this balance is an art, and product managers are the bridge between customer desires and business objectives.

Connecting the Dots

A product team that can seamlessly connect the dots between what they do for the customer and how it serves the broader business mission is one that gains trust and freedom. It's about demonstrating that your product roadmap isn't a collection of features but a strategic journey designed to achieve specific business outcomes. Your roadmap should tell a story of how each feature contributes to the larger narrative of business growth. This narrative is what convinces stakeholders that your team isn't just building features; you're architecting success.

Trust and Freedom

Trust is a precious currency in any organisation. When your product team can articulate how their work directly contributes to the business's success, it builds trust among stakeholders.

This trust, in turn, grants your team the freedom to make informed decisions and navigate their choices confidently. Trust empowers your team to think strategically, take calculated risks, and explore innovative solutions without fear of micromanagement. It's the foundation upon which a culture of autonomy and excellence is built.

Creating Space for Good Product Behaviours

When the alignment between customer value and business objectives is crystal clear, it creates the space for good product behaviours to flourish. These behaviours include a commitment to continuous improvement, experimentation, and innovation, all with a singular focus on delivering meaningful impact. A product culture that values impact encourages a mindset of continuous learning and adaptation. Teams are motivated to experiment, gather data, and iterate based on insights, all in the pursuit of delivering greater value to both customers and the business.

17

Crafting Your Principles

As we've journeyed through the exploration of building a resilient product culture, it's become abundantly clear that culture is not just a lofty concept but a practical and powerful force. We've all heard the adage that "culture eats strategy for breakfast," and in the pursuit of practicality, we've discovered the invaluable role of product principles. These principles are the compass, the guiding light, that makes your culture actionable, memorable, and deeply ingrained in your team's everyday work.

From Concept to Practice

The wisdom gathered during the research for this book emphasised the importance of making culture practical. It's not enough to speak about the virtues of a strong product culture; you must breathe life into it. And the most straightforward way to do that is by crafting a set of product principles—fundamental guidelines and beliefs that serve as the bedrock of your team's behaviour, decision-making, and culture.

Principles: The Practical North Star

Consider principles as a reliable compass that steers decision-making in the tumultuous sea of product development. In the dynamic, ever-shifting realm of product development, principles serve a similar purpose. They are not rigid rules but rather guiding stars that illuminate the path forward.

- **Navigating the Unknown:** Principles become your team's compass when they venture into the often ambiguous and uncertain future of your business and product. They provide clarity in moments of uncertainty, helping your team stay on course.
- **Shaping Behavior and Culture:** Culture is not an abstract concept but a living, breathing entity within your organisation. Principles shape the behaviour and values of your team, guiding their decisions and actions. They become the collective wisdom that drives your team's daily work.
- **Principles in Action:** For instance, a principle might emphasise the importance of user-centricity, reminding your team that every decision should ultimately benefit the end user. Another principle could highlight data-driven decision making, encouraging your team to rely on empirical evidence. Or, a principle might celebrate experimentation and learning, fostering a culture where failure is seen as a stepping stone to success.

Custom-Made for Your Team

Crafting your set of product principles is a deeply personal journey, as unique as your team and your product's mission. It's an opportunity to define the values and beliefs that resonate most deeply with your team's culture and goals.

- **Collective Effort:** Involve your entire team in the process of drafting principles. It's a collaborative endeavour that ensures everyone's voice is heard, creating a sense of ownership and commitment.
- **Clarity and Simplicity:** Keep your principles clear and straightforward. They should be easy to remember and apply in real-world scenarios.
- **Adaptability:** Remember that your principles should not be etched in stone. As your team and product evolve, be open to revisiting and refining your principles to ensure they remain relevant and effective.

Translating Concepts into Principles

To bring the concepts of Quality, Impact, and Urgency to life, you must consider what they mean in your specific context. Write down a set of principles that reflect these values as a guiding light for your teams. These principles will be your North Star as you navigate the unknown future of your business and product, ensuring that your culture isn't just words on paper but a living, breathing force that propels your team forward.

18

Steal Like an Artist

In the captivating book "Steal Like an Artist," Austin Kleon unveils the secrets of the creative process and dispels the myth of the solitary creative genius. He makes a powerful assertion: great art, more often than not, emerges from a combination of inspiration and imitation of the art that has come before it. Kleon's insight is that humans are inherently imperfect, incapable of creating perfect replicas. As they imitate, they introduce their unique imperfections, gradually transforming these imitations into something entirely new and groundbreaking.

A Lesson in Creativity

What's truly remarkable about Kleon's revelation is how applicable it is to the world of product management. Here, too, there's a pervasive myth—a belief in the lone product manager as the solitary genius behind groundbreaking, entirely original products. Yet, the reality is quite different. Just as artists draw inspiration from their predecessors, product managers often begin their journey by borrowing from the wisdom of others, including their product principles.

Borrowing Wisdom

When it comes to crafting your product principles, don't be afraid to start by borrowing. Begin with your first draft and take inspiration from the principles of other companies that resonate with you. Just like a painter learning from the masters, your initial principles may carry echoes of those you admire.

The Practical Path

It's a practical approach to building a foundation for your product culture. By applying borrowed principles in your day-to-day work, you gain insights into what truly resonates with your team and what needs refinement. You're not just copying; you're experimenting, learning, and evolving.

The Evolution of Principles

Over time, as you apply these borrowed principles and adapt them to your unique context, they undergo a transformation. Your team's experiences, challenges, and triumphs infuse them with new life and meaning. What began as imitation becomes a reflection of your team's values, priorities, and aspirations.

Examples to Emulate

To kickstart your journey, take inspiration from companies like GitLab, Amazon and Atlassian, known for their well-defined product principles. Study how they've articulated their guiding beliefs and adapt them to your own needs. It's akin to learning from the classics, understanding the techniques of renowned artists before forging your unique style. Amazon's "Day 1" principle is particularly inspiring to most cultures who want to remain constantly learning and making progress.

Just remember that many creative legends also started this way. Metallica and the Beatles began as cover bands, paying homage to their musical influences. If such an approach was good enough for these legendary sounds, it's certainly worth a try in the realm of product management.

In "Steal Like an Artist," Kleon reminds us that it's not about copying but about embracing the wisdom of those who came before us, infusing it with our unique essence, and letting it evolve into something entirely our own. In the same spirit, as you embark on your journey to define and refine your product principles, remember that you're not just stealing; you're creating, innovating, and shaping a product culture that is uniquely yours—a culture that will inspire your team and drive success in your product endeavours.

19

Write It Down and Share It.

Congratulations on taking the crucial step of crafting your initial set of product principles. However, it's not enough to keep them locked away as your personal treasure. To truly embed these principles into your product culture and let them flourish, you need to write them down and, most importantly, share them with your team.

Testing the Waters with Feedback

Start by sharing your draft with a select group of product team leaders. These are the individuals who are deeply involved in the day-to-day workings of your product, and their insights are invaluable. Ask for their feedback and insights. Does the draft truly reflect the way your team works and the values you want to uphold? Are there gaps or areas that need improvement?

- **Integrating Feedback:** Once you've gathered feedback from

your product team leaders, take the time to integrate and refine their suggestions. This collaborative effort ensures that your principles resonate with those who are actively shaping the product's direction.
- **Expanding the Circle:** With a revised draft in hand, widen your circle of sharing. Include members of your design and engineering teams. These stakeholders play a pivotal role in product development, and their perspectives are essential. Invite their feedback and thoughts on how these principles align with their roles and responsibilities.
- **Iterative Improvement:** Remember that your product principles are a living document. As you share them and gather feedback from various teams, be prepared for iterative improvements. Your principles will evolve and grow stronger with each iteration, becoming a more accurate reflection of your product culture.
- **Building Support:** Sharing your principles in this lean approach has another significant benefit—it helps build support for your product culture. By involving team members at different levels and functions, you create a sense of ownership and alignment. They become active contributors to shaping the culture, rather than passive recipients.

Towards Full Adoption

While you may begin with a select group, the ultimate goal is to share your product principles with everyone in your product organisation. However, the gradual approach of sharing, gathering feedback, and refining ensures that by the time you reach this broader audience, your principles are well-received and resonate with the entire team.

- **The Power of Communication:** Effective communication is at the heart of sharing your principles. Consider hosting meetings or workshops to discuss and explain the principles in detail. Encourage open dialogue and invite questions and discussions. This transparent approach fosters understanding and buy-in.
- **Alignment and Empowerment:** As your principles become deeply ingrained in your product culture, they serve as a source of alignment and empowerment. Team members can refer to them when making decisions, resolving dilemmas, or setting priorities. Your principles become a common language that guides actions.
- **The Journey Continues:** Writing down and sharing your product principles is a pivotal step in shaping a resilient product culture. It's an ongoing journey of refinement and alignment. As your team members embrace these principles and witness their impact on decision-making and outcomes, your product culture will flourish. It's a collective effort, a shared vision, and a journey that promises to elevate your product team to new heights of success.

V

Conclusion

20

Maintaining a Product Culture

Creating a robust product culture is a significant achievement, but the work doesn't end there. Maintaining this culture requires ongoing care and attention. In this chapter, we'll explore the essential practices that ensure your product culture remains strong, vibrant, and aligned with your goals.

Regular Communication and Reinforcement of Values

Consistent communication is the backbone of any successful culture. Regularly share your product principles and the values that underpin your culture with your team. This can take various forms, from team meetings and one-on-one discussions to newsletters or dedicated channels on your communication platforms.

Reinforcement is equally crucial. Celebrate moments when your team embodies these principles, highlighting their importance in real-world scenarios. By consistently weaving these values into your team's conversations and actions, they become second nature.

Encouraging Personal and Professional Growth

A thriving product culture nurtures the growth of its team members. Encourage personal and professional development by providing opportunities for learning, training, and skill enhancement. Invest in courses, workshops, and resources that empower your team to evolve and excel in their roles.

Recognize and support career advancement within your team. When team members see a clear path for growth and development within your organisation, they're more likely to remain engaged and committed.

Fostering a Culture of Learning and Experimentation

Innovation thrives in an environment that embraces learning and experimentation. Encourage your team to explore new ideas and approaches, even if they lead to failures. Failures are valuable lessons that can lead to breakthroughs.

Create safe spaces for experimentation where team members feel empowered to take calculated risks. Encourage them to document what they've learned from both successes and failures, reinforcing the idea that every experience contributes to growth.

Recognizing and Rewarding Success (and Failure)

Recognition is a powerful motivator. Acknowledge and celebrate successes, whether they're small wins or significant milestones. Recognizing achievements not only boosts morale but also reinforces the behaviours and values that contributed to those successes.

Don't shy away from recognizing failures, either. When a well-intentioned effort doesn't yield the expected results, acknowledge it as a learning experience. Discuss what went wrong, what was gained from the experience, and how to improve in the future. This transparency fosters a culture of accountability and resilience.

Continuous Improvement and Evolution

A resilient product culture is one that never rests on its laurels. Encourage a mindset of continuous improvement and evolution. Regularly revisit your product principles and culture as a whole. Are they still aligned with your goals and the changing landscape of your industry? As new people join and as you grow it can be important to revisit these principles and see if they still resonate.

Seek feedback from your team and actively listen to their suggestions for improvement. Embrace change as an opportunity to grow and adapt. A culture that evolves is one that remains relevant and competitive.

21

Appendix - Principles Example

The following are a set of example principles based around our key themes that will give you a good idea of the kind of principles you could develop for your team but please note that these will and should change depending on the kind of organisation you are a part of.

Impact

- **Customer-Business Alignment:** Every decision we make hinges on a dual-axis approach - does it serve our customers' needs and propel our business forward? Balancing these considerations ensures our products make a difference.
- **Impactful Prioritisation**: We strategically prioritise initiatives that promise the most significant positive impact on our customers and yield tangible business outcomes. The 'next big thing' is always anchored in this dual-purpose mindset.

- **Proactive Adaptation**: Rigidity can reduce impact. So, we remain flexible and readily adapt our plans based on customer feedback and market dynamics. It's a careful dance of being customer-oriented while keeping sight of our business goals.

Urgency

- **Prioritised Action**: We employ strategic sequencing of tasks to ensure that the most critical aspects of our work are completed first, optimising the value we deliver.
- **Speed with Foresight**: Though we prioritise swift action, we also recognize the importance of calculated risk-taking and proactively mitigating potential obstacles.
- **Continuous Momentum:** Even when our product has launched, we maintain a high level of urgency to continue refining and improving it, keeping the momentum going beyond day one.

Quality

- **Customer-first Excellence:** Ensuring top-tier quality is non-negotiable because we place our customers at the heart of every decision we make.
- **Reliability in Delivery:** No matter how often we iterate and improve on our products, we strive to deliver secure and

scalable software in a timely manner, without compromising on quality.
- **Evolution without Compromise:** Even in the process of evolving and innovating, we're careful to uphold the high standards of quality that our customers have come to expect from us.

About the Author

As a Director of Product, Simon Hilton is responsible for leading and growing product teams to delight customers. He is also a Mentor at Blackbird Ventures, where he helps startups with product strategy, design, and development. Simon hosts the Product Ops People Podcast, where he interviews guests about their work in product management and operations.

You can connect with me on:
🌐 https://www.simonhilton.co

Also by Simon Hilton

The Product Ops Pillars

Product Ops Pillars is the first book to provide an accessible summary of what modern Product Operations looks like. You'll learn how to improve your team's performance and efficiency, which tools are essential, and how to design an operating model that will keep your company on top.

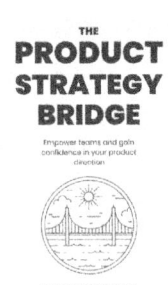

The Product Strategy Bridge

Product Strategy Bridge is a practical guidebook that provides a comprehensive approach to product strategy. In this book, the authors Alejandro Patterson and Simon Hilton, offer a step-by-step framework for aligning product strategy with business goals and execution.

Printed in Great Britain
by Amazon